PLANET EARTH

GLACIERS

Big
Buddy BOOKS
Planet Earth

ABDO
Publishing Company

Marcia Zappa

VISIT US AT
www.abdopublishing.com

Published by ABDO Publishing Company, 8000 West 78th Street, Edina, Minnesota 55439.

Copyright © 2011 by Abdo Consulting Group, Inc. International copyrights reserved in all countries. No part of this book may be reproduced in any form without written permission from the publisher. Big Buddy Books™ is a trademark and logo of ABDO Publishing Company.

Printed in the United States of America, North Mankato, Minnesota.
032010
092010

 PRINTED ON RECYCLED PAPER

Coordinating Series Editor: Rochelle Baltzer
Contributing Editors: Heidi M.D. Elston, Megan M. Gunderson, BreAnn Rumsch, Sarah Tieck
Graphic Design: Adam Craven
Cover Photograph: *Shutterstock*: Pablo H. Caridad.
Interior Photographs/Illustrations: *AP Photo*: Alexander Colhoun (p. 5); *Corbis*: © Arctic-Images (p. 19),
    © Fred Hirschmann/Science Faction (pp. 11, 25), © Galen Rowell (p. 17) © Paul A. Souders (p. 25); *Getty
    Images*: Doug Allan (p. 9); Image Science and Analysis Laboratory, NASA-Johnson Space Center (p. 13);
    NASA (p. 5); *Peter Arnold, Inc.*: © Biosphoto/BIOS; Bios-Auteurs (droits geres); Bringard Denis (p. 25),
    Nick Cobbing (p. 27), Bryan Lynas (p. 15), Alan Majchrowicz (p. 13), Jim Wark (p. 7); *Photo Researchers,
    Inc.*: Michael P. Gadomski (p. 23), Science Source (p. 5); *Shutterstock*: Adrian Coroama (p. 16), deckard_73
    (p. 21), JJ pixs (p. 21), Ales Liska (p. 25), Oleg_Mit (p. 29), PSD Photography (p. 30), Eduardo Rivero
    (p. 5).

Library of Congress Cataloging-in-Publication Data

Zappa, Marcia.
  Glaciers / Marcia Zappa.
    p. cm. -- (Planet Earth)
  ISBN 978-1-61613-493-8
  1. Glaciers--Juvenile literature. I. Title.
  GB2403.8.Z37 2010
  551.31'2--dc22
                    2009053195

TABLE OF CONTENTS

AN IMPORTANT ELEMENT

What important features come to mind when you think of planet Earth? Lots of people think of rocks, water, and soil. But what about ice?

Ice forms huge masses called glaciers. Glaciers cover about 10 percent of Earth's land. They form in cold areas. They slowly move over land, changing the surface. Glaciers are an important part of planet Earth.

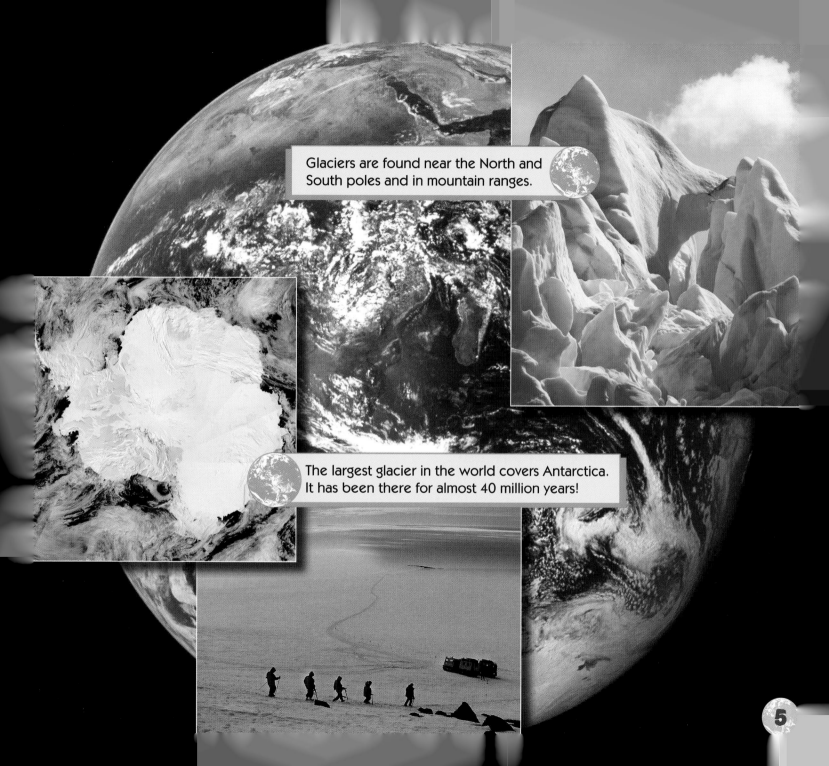

Glaciers are found near the North and South poles and in mountain ranges.

The largest glacier in the world covers Antarctica. It has been there for almost 40 million years!

SNOW PILES

Some parts of Earth have temperatures so cold that snow never fully melts. Over many years, the snow piles up.

As the snow piles higher, it presses down on the bottom layers. They are pressed so hard that they turn into ice. Glaciers form in these areas.

The largest glacier in North America is Alaska's Malaspina Glacier. It is more than 50 miles (80 km) long!

SCIENCE SPOT

Glaciers shrink and grow with changing temperatures. Warm temperatures cause glaciers to melt and shrink. Cool temperatures prevent this. When it snows, glaciers in cool temperatures grow.

SCIENCE SPOT

Glaciers are also grouped according to their temperature. Temperate glaciers stay at or near a temperature that could melt them. Polar glaciers stay much colder.

ALL SHAPES AND SIZES

There are many different types of glaciers. They are grouped based on location, size, and shape. The two main types are continental glaciers and mountain glaciers.

Continental glaciers are also called ice sheets.

SHEETS OF ICE

Continental glaciers are wide, thick sheets of ice. They cover most of Antarctica and Greenland. These glaciers build up in the center. They slope down at the edges.

Continental glaciers can be more than two miles (3 km) thick! They often cover the land completely.

Sometimes, continental glaciers cover all the land except tall mountain peaks. These peaks are known as nunataks.

SCIENCE SPOT

Ice caps are another type of glacier. They have shapes similar to continental glaciers. But, ice caps are smaller.

11

LONG AND LEAN

Mountain glaciers exist in many forms. One common type is a valley glacier. Valley glaciers are often long and narrow. They are found in mountain ranges all over the world.

Some mountain glaciers form at the base of a mountain. There, they can spread out onto flat land. They take on the shape of a round lump. These are called piedmont (PEED-mahnt) glaciers.

Valley glaciers may appear to be in warm locations. But at the tops of high mountains, air remains cold enough for glaciers.

Some large piedmont glaciers form when several valley glaciers meet at a mountain's base.

13

LAWS OF GRAVITY

Glaciers move because of gravity. Gravity is a natural force that pulls objects to the ground. This force is always pulling glaciers down.

Sometimes, gravity pulls glaciers across land. Friction and Earth's heat cause the bottom of a glacier to melt slightly. That makes it slippery, allowing the glacier to slide over land.

Gravity pulls mountain glaciers down mountainsides.

15

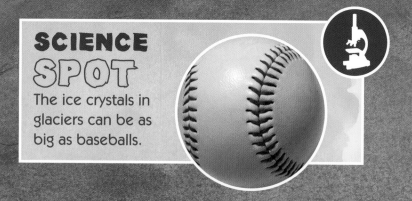

Other times, changes inside glaciers cause them to move. Glaciers are made up of ice crystals. Gravity can pull down on a glacier so hard its crystals change shape. This change makes the glacier **shift**.

When water freezes, it forms a pattern of 3–D shapes. These shapes are called ice crystals.

SLOW AND STEADY

Glaciers move at different speeds. Most move very slowly. They may move less than one inch (3 cm) each year!

Some glaciers go through fast-moving periods. These are called surges. Surges may last several weeks to a few years. The fastest glacier surge ever recorded lasted three months. The glacier moved about 300 feet (90 m) a day!

Surges can cause glaciers to crack and break apart.

19

EARTH MOVERS

Glaciers are powerful forces in shaping Earth's surface. They are very heavy. Glaciers move like bulldozers, knocking down **landforms** and trees. They even scrape away mountainsides.

Sometimes, glaciers create deep, thin valleys that reach the ocean. These are called fjords. This happens when glaciers carve deep into land near the ocean. After the glacier melts, the valley fills with seawater.

In Yosemite National Park in California, ancient glaciers cut away mountainsides. They created deep valleys with steep walls.

Glaciers collect sediment as they move. These sharp objects can wear away rock as glaciers push them over it.

Melting glaciers often leave behind sediment. Sometimes, it piles up to make new landforms, such as hills.

Lines scratched into rock by glaciers are called striations.

23

WHAT'S LEFT BEHIND

Certain glacier movements create special **landforms**. The landforms add to Earth's natural beauty. They teach scientists about glaciers that existed long ago.

CIRQUES

ARÊTES

Arêtes (uh-RAYTS) are sharp ridges on mountainsides. They are created when two glaciers move down a mountain on opposite sides.

HORNS

Horns are steep, pointed peaks. They form when three or more glaciers carve away a mountain on different sides.

Sediments pushed or carried by a glacier tend to pile up around its edges. When a glacier melts, the sediments can form narrow mounds called moraines.

MORAINES

25

MELTING GLACIERS

Earth's glaciers are slowly melting. Scientists believe this is because of a **climate** change called global warming.

Melting glaciers have harmful effects on Earth. Glaciers hold a lot of water in the form of ice. When they melt, the water enters the oceans. Rising oceans can cause low land areas to flood. They can also cause storms, **droughts**, and other **extreme** weather.

If all of Earth's glaciers melted, the oceans would rise about 250 feet (80 m).

SCIENCE SPOT

Global warming is an increase in Earth's surface temperature. It is caused mostly from air pollution. Some cars and businesses create harmful gases. As these gases fill the air, they trap heat. This causes the temperature to rise.

People are working to limit global warming. You can help too! Ride a bike instead of riding in a car. Use reusable shopping bags instead of plastic store bags. Help your family plant a tree. These actions will help keep Earth a beautiful place!

Glaciers are an important part of Earth's natural wonder!

DOWN TO EARTH:
A FEW MORE FACTS ABOUT GLACIERS

- Glaciers can range from several feet to more than 10,000 feet (3,000 m) thick!
- Some glaciers flow toward oceans. When a chunk of glacier falls into the water, it is called calving (*right*). The chunks are called icebergs.
- Earth's climate has changed throughout history. During cold periods with heavy snow, continental glaciers covered large areas of land. These periods are known as ice ages. The last ice age ended about 11,700 years ago.

IMPORTANT WORDS

climate the weather and temperatures that are normal in a certain place.

drought (DRAUT) a long period of dry weather.

extreme (ihk-STREEM) far beyond the usual.

friction (FRIHK-shuhn) a force that slows motion when two surfaces touch each other.

landform a natural feature of a land surface. Hills and mountains are types of landforms.

sediment bits of materials, such as rocks or sand, moved by water, wind, and glaciers.

shift to make a change in place, position, or direction.

temperature (TEHM-puhr-chur) the measured level of hot or cold.

WEB SITES

To learn more about glaciers, visit ABDO Publishing Company online. Web sites about glaciers are featured on our Book Links page. These links are routinely monitored and updated to provide the most current information available.

www.abdopublishing.com

INDEX